Help God!!
My Children Need New Parents!

By Brenda Billingy, M.Ed.

Dedications

To all parents struggling to maintain your sanity as you attempt to train your children to become productive adults.

To my husband who helped to preserve my sanity during those years.

To the "sisters in the village" who graciously shared their wisdom and encouragement and kept hope alive!

CHAPTER 1
TEENAGE DILEMMA

Teenagers – I was one a very long time ago – but it didn't seem like such a challenging age. I must have been "the perfect teenager" (at least so I thought) until close friends reminded me otherwise. I loved being a parent. I sacrificed my career to be a stay-at-home Mom. I realized that I had only one chance to do parenting right. Once the years pass, they can never be recalled or redone.

However, no one can really prepare you for parenting teenagers. It's like pregnancy – you can read all about it, talk to others about it, visualize yourself in it, but the true reality hits when you really become pregnant! Dealing with different personalities in your children also poses an interesting dilemma, for then you are forced to become "multiple persons in one." Certain statements became part of our everyday conversations: "you never let us go…My friend's Mom doesn't see anything wrong with…Why can't I?…You guys are the only parents in the world who are…I can't wait until I'm old enough…"

One challenge per day would be difficult enough, but at times they seemed to come in waves, and on those days I understood what it meant to pray without ceasing. However, I knew I was becoming desperate when one day I locked myself in my closet upon hearing the heavy stomping of my daughter approaching my room. That was my warning to put on the whole armor of God, pray and be prepared for warfare. She found me in the closet with a tension-filled question. "Mom could I….?" "I'm sorry, you can't….." and the war was on! After being in combat zone for about 15 minutes, and battle-weary at best, I locked myself again in the closet to agonize with God.

"Help God! My children need new parents!! I don't know how you will do it, but I need a replacement very soon. I've done my best so far – but these teenage years are more than I can handle. You responded to ordinary people in scripture when they called for help – even performing miracles if necessary. I don't know what I'm asking – or what I'm expecting, but I do know that I need your divine intervention!" After a while the room was quiet, the house was still, and taking a deep breath I dared to reenter the child-rearing ring again.

Diversions are always helpful and healthy. They temporarily remove your mind from the mundane issues of life as you get absorbed in your present activity. For me car washing is an excellent diversion. Maybe it's the clean, fluffy soap suds that serve as a refreshing symbol of hope. With a good wash we can all be made clean, dirt can be removed and we can start all over again as renewed vessels. Engrossed in this spiritual thought, I was enjoying the prospect of spiritual cleanliness with the water of the Spirit when a weird thought interrupted my brain waves.

"Brenda, it's time to give up your children – release them – don't hold on to them any longer – let them know it today."

"But Lord, how can I do that? They are only teenagers. They are not going anywhere anytime soon." But oftentimes God will only speak once. He knows you heard and He expects you to obey. After all, it's the same method of operation I took with my children. So with dirty rag in hand, I hesitatingly mentioned to my husband that we should schedule a family meeting later that night. It was time to let the kids go. Go where? I wasn't sure, but I do know I needed to release them.

Maybe I was the only family member feeling the tension of this meeting – probably since I had no detailed plans. My personality profile requires that I always have detailed plans – without them I'm slightly uncomfortable. But the meeting had already convened and all inquiring minds wanted to know…What's the agenda? I can't quite remember the words I mumbled, but I do remember saying that "I've given you the best years of my life – I've done all I can do, said all I can say. Anything else will be repetitious. Now I must release you, and pray that the Lord will help you to make good decisions and wise choices."

My warrior looked at me with a slight smile. She must have been thinking – "it's about time Mom, finally you've seen the light." Neither of us knew at that moment what these words meant or what the process of release would entail, but we were weary enough to give God a chance at coming up with a fresh new peaceable idea. I determined to leave the table with at least a mental peace treaty intact. I would simply await further instructions from God.

CHAPTER 2
ABSORBING THE WORD

God gave me what I consider to be an exciting spiritual habit – that of tearing texts apart simply by looking up the meaning of each word in the dictionary and then rewriting the text according to the "everyday" meaning of the words.

On the morning of November 2, 1992, I decided to dismantle Philipians 4:7: "Be careful for nothing, but in everything by prayer and supplication with thanksgiving let your requests be made known unto God. And the peace of God that passeth all understanding shall keep your hearts and minds through Christ Jesus." Following are the dictionary meanings and Brenda's translation.

BE - future Action

CAREFUL - mental distress, worry, concern

FOR - indicates appropriateness

NOTHING - in no way or degree, not anything

BUT - on the contrary

EVERYTHING - all factors or things with no exception

BY - through the means or agency of

PRAYER - an earnest plea when there is minimal chance or hope

SUPPLICATION - to ask humbly, earnest appeal

WITH - including, at the same time as

THANKSGIVING - expressing gratitude or appreciation

LET - to allow

REQUESTS - to ask someone to do something

KNOWN - make a party to confidential or special information

GOD - the One who possesses supernatural powers

PEACE – serenity, calm

PASSETH - goes beyond

UNDERSTANDING - ability to comprehend, perceive

SHALL – inevitable, cannot be prevented

KEEP - provide maintenance & support to continue your course

HEARTS - mood and disposition

MINDS - thoughts, desires, purposes, sanity

THROUGH - by means of

CHRIST - The Messiah, Jesus

BRENDA'S   TRANSLATION

"In the future, note that it really is not appropriate for you to allow anything to cause you worry, concern or mental distress. On the contrary, in all conditions, even when there is minimal chance or hope- allow the Ruler of the Universe to be privy to all personal, confidential and special things that you would like him to do. Let Him know this through the agency of earnest and humble appeals, and at the same time don't forget to express your gratitude and appreciation to Him.

And this God who possesses supernatural powers will, as a result of your requests, give you a calm serenity beyond anyone's ability to comprehend. Inevitably He will support and maintain your moods, dispositions, as well as your thoughts, desires and stated purposes – even your sanity is preserved. How will all this be accomplished? Only through the authority of the Messiah – Jesus Christ."

Isn't it a joy to know that the battle you face today is not really yours – it's the Lord's!! I was so excited over the fact that God had most of the work to do, that I decided to review my tasks again to be sure that I didn't miss any steps. It seemed that whenever problems arose, all I needed to do was devote myself to PRAYER, SUPPLICATION and THANKSGIVING. Prayer and supplication seemed almost one in the same, but there must be a reason why they are listed separately. This called for another excavation trip to the dictionary.

PRAYER: To request with earnest, humble entreaty. To obtain by begging or bring about by praying.
    Request – expressing desire for something
    Earnest – serious, intense, important
    Entreat – to persuade by imploring or beseeching

SUPPLICATION: to humbly request by way of a **petition**
    Petition – earnest request to a superior in authority. Presented in <u>formal writing</u> or <u>document</u> embodying such a request signed by petitioners. Specific action is asked for formally.

THANKSGIVING: a formal, often public, expression of appreciation or gratitude. Grateful acknowledgement of something received by or done for you.

There it was – my three tasks – Prayer and Thanksgiving seemed easy enough, but for the first time I was presented with this notion of a written **petition.** God added a little more "bait" by referring me to 1 John 5:14, 15 – "And this is the confidence that we have in him, that, if we ask anything according to his will, he heareth us. And if we know that he hears us, whatsoever we ask, we know that we have the **petition** that we desired of him."

There is nothing more exciting than to discover a guarantee in Scripture. Ask in His will – He will hear – We will receive. Really, could it be that simple? I was now determined to find out. Inquiring minds need to know. Who would be the best person to give me further specifics on **petitions.** An attorney maybe – yes, and I knew one who could quickly brief me by phone (It's good to have friends in high places).

The phone rang and I completely bypass the trivial, mundane "hello, how are you" and skipped right to – "tell me in brief, what does a **petition** entail?" The descriptive answer was a bit complicated, so I asked if she could send me something in writing. Free of charge, I received the following:

PETITION:
A written address (document) *embodying a request or prayer* (it's actually called a prayer in legal terms) *signed by the*

person or persons preferring it, to the superior power or person to whom it is presented, for the exercise of his or their authority in the redress of some wrong, or the grant of some favor, privilege or license.

An application in writing for an order of the court, stating the circumstances upon which it is founded. Petitions may in some cases be presented by persons not parties to the case.

An application made to a court ex parte, or where there are no parties in opposition, praying for the exercise of the judicial powers of the court in relation to some matter which is not the subject for a suit or action, or for authority to do some act which requires the sanction of the court.

Wow!!! A **petition** seems to be a very "legal" thing. It involves written documents, court, and a judge. The only question remaining was – What physical problem am I now experiencing that I would like to be rid of? How could I frame a **petition** to God that could present this problem to Him in a spiritual manner? Oops – my closet prayer flashed across my mind– "Help God, my children need new parents! Can you please adopt them and release me of the responsibility?" Maybe I can present this problem to God in a formal adoption petition.

Hoping that my friend would not be too tired of my vague questions, I got back on the phone with another request. I needed to know how one should go about preparing an adoption **petition.** She was wiser this time and said that rather than attempting to explain it to me, it would probably make more sense to take a look at an actual legal adoption request. She would then explain all that was included in the process so that I could follow along carefully. Creativity is an indelible teacher. If something is taught in a creative manner, it tends to stick with me better. Jesus was extremely creative. On a Sabbath day, rather than just preaching and singing a hymn, He would teach parables in the open air. When He needed money for taxes, rather than reach for his money pouch, he told his disciples to go fishing and find the money in the mouth of a fish. By so doing, He was teaching creative lessons – lessons that would forever remind them of the Power of Jesus. I sensed Jesus was once again crafting a creative teaching mechanism, one that I would never forget. He could simply command that I entrust my children into his care, or He could give me the task of creating a formal adoption ***petition*** to be presented to Him in earnest prayer. He chose the latter. The ball was now in my court – and just how would I ever begin to prepare an adoption ***petition?***

CHAPTER 3
HOMEWORK

"Sorry to call again, K, but what would be the most important guideline in this preparation process?"

"Well, whenever I have to present a petition in court, the first thing I do is try to get to know the 'mind' of the Judge, and that's easily done by researching how he has ruled in similar cases and what was required for such favorable ruling."

From the biblical references I had seen in the past, I was sure that God was in favor of adoption. He even said we could call Him Abba, Father. That's a plus – hopefully He would say YES to adopting my girls (the Bible did say that all God's promises are YES and AMEN).

On that positive note, I set out to do my research – getting to know the mind of the Judge, with His assurance that as I go through this process: (1) I would feel closer to God because of the huge amount of preparation time needed, (2) I would become more confident in prayer (you can really come boldly before the throne when you know the mind of the Judge and you are prepared to approach Him appropriately), (3) If I spent all that time doing research, it would force me to act in faith – believing God's word.

What would <u>believing</u> have to do with preparing a document? I had no idea of the magnitude of this project, nor the faith that would be required to see it to completion. But I was about to find out!

2 Chronicles 20 was my first study – read this fascinating story yourself. God's creative teaching is amazing, but the faith requirement was even more astounding! When we take our eyes off ourselves and place them on God, as the children of Judah did, and come to Him for the answer to our problems, then we have a right to claim what God has promised. It is simply because the promise was made by God, and He cannot lie! He is able to fulfill His word. "Believe" was the burden of the message of Jehoshaphat to his people. He wanted to impress upon them the fact that this message had come from the Lord based on His promises, but belief was primary – without it there could be no success. It is still very true for us today.

When should we express or demonstrate our belief? When we begin to see evidences of Him solving the problem? No, it should be before you see any external evidences. This is a difficult position to assume, and it's the point where we often fail. Jehoshaphat had his CHOIR go before the ARMY singing the victory song BEFORE they engaged in battle. Now this may have seemed backward – wars are not won by choirs, and most victory songs are sung after the battle is over and the victory is actually won. But this creative endeavor fulfilled the last part of the text which linked supplication with Thanksgiving, and the Bible says *"when they began to sing, the Lord began to move"*. The enemies began to fight against each other and eventually destroyed one another. God came to their aid when they asked for His help; when they affirmed their belief in His promise by moving forward; and when they claimed the answer by giving thanks as though they had already received it.

This was faith in action – naked faith – the substance of things hoped for, but the evidence of things not seen. Believing before any indication was given that the answer would come. Believing no matter how "crazy" God's commands may seem. Trusting God's Word <u>ONLY</u> is a habit that must be developed if we are to experience the miracles of God in our lives.

There is no logic to this operation – no method to the madness. If they had been using only common sense someone would have said "Hey folks, lets back off here. We don't have enough fighting power, our soldiers haven't had a scrimmage in a while, we haven't had our traditional morning devotion or sung the appropriate "plea for mercy" song. *Common sense will keep you bound when its time to act in faith on God's word.* You may try to reason things out in your head, but reasoning outside the Word of God leads to worry and our text already admonishes us not to worry – Be careful for nothing – but if the problem is big enough and heavy enough that you know it is beyond your strength and ability, then God says come with prayer, supplication/ petition with thanksgiving, and while He is working it out He will give you peace. *When you need more than just common sense results, faith is the only way you will get it.*

The children of Judah truly learned that day how to pray in the Will of God – according to the mind of God. Allow me to correct a notion that has plagued our church for years. We have been taught to always pray "Lord IF it is Your will," and that's valid. But here is what that does NOT mean:

(1) The IF in that statement does not infer IGNORANCE. When Jesus prayed "Father if this be your will, let this cup pass," it was not that he didn't know what God's will was for his life. He knew the assigned task at hand. He knew what was expected of Him. His "IF" included absolute knowledge of God's will.

(2) Praying in the Will of God does not mean that you bring God your agenda items – vocalize them and then at the end tag on the phrase, "Lord please grant me these requests if it is your will." That's a cop out – it's a prayer blanket that we throw over our prayers and hope that they would stay warm and germinate into reality. If God doesn't answer as we expected, we wouldn't be too embarrassed because, after all, we can then say "Well, it wasn't God's will anyway."

But God is calling us to graduate from the pediatrics of prayer. He wants us to study, know His mind, His will – remind Him of His promises as it relates to your needs. Delight yourself in the Lord and then He will give you the desires of your heart. For something to become a delight, you've got to spend a lot of time with it – almost to the point where it becomes a part of you. My husband and I have been married now for over 35 years and I can say that we delight in each other (most of the time anyway). We know each other's mind and how it functions. Similarly, when you become so tight with God, you know His mind – His will becomes your will, and you will discover that your prayers begin to line up with His will, having the assurance that God cannot lie.

From this study I was convinced that if I became familiar with the promises of God, I could then present my request for adoption of my children according to the mind of the Judge (God). As long as those two are one in the same, my prayers will be heard, and I will receive the help I needed. But do I believe? Do I have faith? I was grateful to find in Scripture that God has given to every man a measure of faith, and that even if it is as small as a mustard seed, I can still move mountains. "Yes Lord, I believe. Help thou my unbelief." I'm determined to be a believer!

CHAPTER 4
THE VILLAGE

People have always said that it takes a village to raise a child. At that point I was convinced that there was an error in that statement – they really should have said that it takes "several" villages to raise a child. I knew this project was too big for me to handle on my own, and I had the urgent feeling that God wanted others to share in it. I was grateful for any company or villages willing to share and support. So with paper and pen in hand I sat down to listen to God's voice. I couldn't choose the names myself – it was strictly God's choice. Before long, I had written the names of nine other mothers – I don't know why God chose them, but it seemed that we all had one thing in common – raising children around the same ages – the best way we knew how.

What do I say to them Lord? How do you present such a 'weird' idea to sane people without having them think that you are weird? Again, desperation was a motivating factor. I dialed one phone number after another, letting the Moms know that they were selected by God to partner with me in this process. Just what were we going to accomplish? We are presenting to God a formal petition asking Him to adopt our children and free us from our parental responsibility. NOT ONE MOM SAID NO!! We would form our own village of **Petition Mothers** determined to do battle in prayer for our children. Ellen G. White states that "Heaven always responds to the call of a soul. It is pledged to do so and will fulfill the promise, so the prayers which are ascending daily are as sure to be answered as the truth is sure that God's throne is eternal. The last mediatorial work of Christ before laying aside His priest's robe is to present the **prayers of parents for their children.** And I saw a mighty angel sent out and thousands of children will remember their training and be brought back before probation closes." Review & Herald,1980.

The following week I sent out an urgent letters to all the Moms giving them the background of the petition idea and inviting them to participate in a petition-signing ceremony to be held on Friday July 29, 1994. The following excerpts from the letter indicates the serious impression of the Holy Spirit on this project:

"writing this letter is a real task, but one thing is for sure – this is a God-given assignment and its probably the most serious thing I have written yet. I have asked the Lord to show me who I should mail this letter to and I pray that you would grasp the seriousness of it as you read. This assignment will require some work and faith effort on your part. IF YOU DISCOVER THAT YOU DO NOT HAVE THE TIME TO COMPLETE THIS ASSIGNMENT FULLY, OR IF YOU FEEL DOUBT IN YOUR HEART, PLEASE – PLEASE DO NOT FEEL PRESSURED TO ATEND THE SESSION OUTLINED. THIS IS FOR SERIOUS PARTICIPANTS ONLY!! You are invited to a private, special petition-signing ceremony to be held on Friday July 29th at 8:00 PM. On this evening we will be formally presenting our Petition for Adoption to the Lord. There are a few things to be done in preparation for this day. Any attorney will tell you that 'ONE UNPREPARED WITNESS CAN DO SERIOUS DAMAGE TO A COURT CASE' and this is much too serious to risk damaging this **petition**."

I could only imagine the responses to this letter! Maybe the negative feedback would come sooner than I thought! But surprise, surprise – every Mom called back excited and determined to complete all assignments. I guess the village was experiencing the same problems and looking for the same answers as it relates to raising children. The homework assignments involved serious study of Biblical texts related to children- (e.g. Isaiah 54:13, Acts 16:31, Matthew 18:14, Jeremiah 2:9), prayer and fasting sessions, and shared devotional readings on Faith.

These however, were not just reading exercises, they were designed to instill strong faith and confident trust that what God says He will do – He will do. Faith cometh (increaseth) by hearing the Word of God, and it did for each mother. Every day the phones would be buzzing with the sharing of exciting promises and amazing discoveries! God was definitely with us, and we were all anxious to see what He would do. Thankful for the support, I took on the major task of preparing and rewriting legal adoption documents into spiritual language. If this was going to be a creative process, we should go all out! (At that time I had no idea what "all out" would mean!)

CHAPTER 5
RENAMING OUR CHILDREN

In researching the adoption process, I quickly discovered that one of the first assignments of the adoptive parents is to rename the adopted children. In Biblical times, parents chose the names of their children very carefully – it was usually based on the direction that they wanted their child to take, or it signified/ highlighted some spiritual aspect of the child's life (names were changed even after many years of life – e.g. Sarai to Sarah or Abram to Abraham). The Lord impressed me that if He had to adopt our children they would have to be renamed with biblical names, according to the spiritual direction we would like for each child and based on their unique personalities. I called the Moms to let them know that they had one additional assignment – research the biblical name you would like your child to adopt. This name should be one that suits their personality and indicates the spiritual direction for their lives. What a unique challenge! But I was confident that the Bible had enough names for everyone. Once a name was selected, a thorough research of that biblical character had to be conducted. Each mom listed valid reasons as to why she wanted such a name change in the presentation of the **petition.** It was fun trying to fit your child into the life of a Bible character.

Finding names for both my girls was not too difficult. Neither of them possessed any type of "blended" personality. However, I had an additional challenge. Over the years, the Lord brought me two young men, both of whom had no Adventist parents. They were the only ones in their families who joined the Adventist faith at an early age. Meeting each young man separately, I was instantly impressed that they were to become my spiritual sons. As Pharoah's daughter did for Moses, I took them under my spiritual wing and began teaching, encouraging, mentoring, supporting these two young men as though they were my own. Should I include them in this **petition** as my own children? The answer was "Yes." Now I had to research two boys' names – something I hadn't done in real life. Even though it felt odd, researching boys' names and matching them with personalities actually gave me the "feel" of being a real mother to them. All of a sudden I had four children!! Oh dear – adoption couldn't have come at a better time!

Moms were quite excited about this process – everyone wanted to be sure that the names fit their children's personality perfectly, yet with a biblical twist. Some chose several names and then went through a process of elimination. The question for the week was- "so what's your child's new name going to be?" It was a delightful surprise to discover that a few mothers who had children with similar personalities chose the same biblical name for their adoption. Same personality – same spiritual name! We interpreted that to be God's confirmation that those names were the right ones for those children. Once we settled on the names, each Mom then wrote a short synopsis of the Bible character, and why they wanted that name to be the new spiritual name for their child when he/she was adopted by the Lord. Since God was going to be the new parent, we felt we should select a new last name for the children that would reflect His character and what He would be willing to do for them as a new parent. The most appropriate and important thing God has done for our children was to redeem them. Therefore we agreed that all our children will now have the last name "Redeemed." Following is an example of the new name selected for one of my daughters:

Esther Faith Redeemed

ESTHER - Beautiful in heart, courageous, independent. Following God's plan to reverse evil. Not following the crowd. Acting with conviction. Close to her family. Rising to leadership. God used her to accomplish extraordinary things.

> STUDY - The Book of Esther, Isaiah 50:7, Eph. 3:20, Phil. 4:6,7,13, Deut. 28:13,14, Deut. 30:19, Deut. 31:6, Rom. 12:2, James 1:5.

FAITH - Loyalty to principles and beliefs. Trustworthy – show allegiance and unquestioned belief in God. To know that God is reliable. To demonstrate confidence, sincerity and honesty.

> STUDY- Job 2:3, Psalm 26:1, Prov. 19:1, Prov. 20:7, Rom. 10:17, Psalm 125:1, 1 John 5:4, Deut. 31:8.

REDEEMED - Referenced from Isaiah 43:1. God will fulfill this promise to you, because he has already rescued, recovered and bought you back with the precious sacrifice that delivers you from sin. Because He has already made atonement for you, we can expect that you will become a new person – a true convert.

ESTHER: I PLAN TO SEE YOU WEAR YOUR CROWN IN HEAVEN!! WE HAVE TO BE THERE TOGETHER AS A FAMILY!

One of the English meanings for the name Esther is "a star." No better name could describe this particular child. She was born to be an Esther – always getting people out of trouble and looking out for others. A loyal faithful friend she is indeed. So what's in a name? As you can tell, it's a whole lot! We wanted each name to indicate the blessings and direction we were asking the Lord to provide for each life. Every Mom had to be satisfied that their child was covered and would be well taken care of, therefore much effort went into the selection of new names for our children and we claimed the scripture promises associated with those names. This all seemed like a dream, and the deeper we got into this project the more faith was needed to BELIEVE that God would actually hear us and answer our prayers for adoption.

CHAPTER 6

SETTING A COURT DATE

"Since you are reviewing court documents and applying them to the children, why don't you go all the way and actually make a formal presentation in a court setting?" I jumped – who's speaking? Did I hear that voice correctly? – a formal court presentation? I knew we would come together as a group at some point in time – but I thought it would be just for prayer for the children. I was not quite prepared for this level of faith walking – but I had started something and by the Holy Spirit I needed to complete it. I allowed by mind to follow and take careful notes of the Spirit's suggestions:

- Find a room that could be set us as a courtroom
- Set an official date that the Moms would appear in court
- Someone should be prepared to present the case (spiritual attorney)
- Each Mom should be prepared to take the witness stand and plead their case
- Children should be briefed regarding the fact that they will be presented for adoption, and have opportunity to study their new name and meaning
- Dads should lead out in this process with children
- Fast and prayer during the week of the adoption procedure
- Prepare official courtroom proceedings involving Prayer, Supplication/Petition and Thanksgiving sessions
- Prepare official adoption documents for each child
- Share all confirmations of this procedure with Moms.

Obviously I had bitten off much more than I could chew. Not only was this task enormous, but I could also appear quite foolish to the ears of those who did not receive this word firsthand. But this could not be just a game, not just a creative exercise, something about this seemed so serious, that I was actually scared NOT to obey. I prayed that day telling the Lord that I would be obedient, but He has to do the work, because I didn't have a clue how I should begin putting these documents together. I picked up my pen and paper early the next morning and the Lord himself began to write. I could tell immediately, that it was going to be my assignment to be the attorney for the group. Not only must I prepare the adoption papers, but I must also prepare an argument that will be convincing to the judge to grant this adoption request. My friend's advice resounded in my head like a bell – "To win a case, you should seek to know the mind of the judge (what he has said or done in the past in similar cases) and then prepare your argument according to his mindset." I had to search the scriptures for promises God had already given and construct my presentation based on His promises only. After all, we are assured that His word will not return void, but will accomplish the thing for which it was sent. This is one court case I needed to win! Following is the official document translated into spiritual language in preparation for the presentation to the judge on the assigned court date – July 29, 1994.

SUPERIOR COURT OF
THE CITY OF HEAVEN
FAMILY DIVISION

EX PARTE IN THE MATTER OF
THE PETITION OF

_____(Parent)
Adoption No. _7_   (Perfection)

FOR ADOPTION OF

_____ (Child)
_____ (Child)
_____ (Child)
_____ (Child)

PETITION FOR ADOPTION

The attorney in this case is Brenda Billingy and the Petitioners are all witnesses agreed hereto. The Petitioner(s) represent(s) to this Heavenly Court:

1. That this court has jurisdiction of this proceeding under the provisions of the Creation Code, Genesis Sec. 1 & 2 in that:
   - The Petitioner(s) is/are legally residents of this world.

- The prospective adoptee is in the legal care of my family – a child-placing agency licensed by my church.

2. If married: the Petitioner's spouse is a joint party to this petition.

3. All information which is required pursuant to the Creation Code & Birth is appended to this Petition in the Statement of Information.

4. An adoption blessing agreement has not been entered into prior to the filing of this Petition.

5. The prospective adoptee is physically, mentally and otherwise suitable for adoption.

6. The Petitioner's is/are fit and able to give the prospective adoptee a proper home and education.

7. The adoption is in the best interest of the prospective adoptee.

8. The Petitioner's desire(s) to have conferred upon the prospective adoptee that same status of parent(s) and child for all purposes between the Redeemer and the prospective adoptee.

9. That the name(s) of the adoptee(s) be changed.

10. For such other and further relief as may seem just and proper to the Heavenly Court.

JULY 29, 1994

_____ (Petitioner)
Being first sworn, testify that I have read the Petition for Adoption and understand its terms and believe that the statements contained in this Petition are true.

SUPERIOR COURT OF
THE CITY OF HEAVEN
FAMILY DIVISION

EX PARTE IN THE MATTER OF THE
ADOPTION PETITION OF

_____ (Parent)
Adoption No. 7 (Perfection)

PETITION FOR ADOPTION:
STATEMENT OF INFORMATION

PETITIONER

Name: _____
Spouse: _____
Address: _____

PROSPECTIVE ADOPTEE(S):

Name: _____
Sex: _____ Age: _____

Name: _____
Sex: _____ Age: _____

Name: _____
Sex: _____ Age: _____

Name: _____
Sex: _____   Age: _____

The prospective adoptee is in the legal care and custody of Parents:

        0 Yes   0 No

Consent for adoption has been obtained from
Spouse: 0 Yes   0 No
Adoptee(s):   0 Yes   0 No

Natural parents are willing to relinquish parental rights to the Supernatural Redeemer:

        0 Yes   0 No

<u>July 29, 1994</u>

_____(Petitioner)

Subscribe and sworn to before me
Attorney
Deputy Clerk/Acting Notary Public

CHAPTER 7

COURTROOM PROCEEDINGS FOR JULY 29

JUDGE'S CHAMBERS: (PRAYER)

- Review Jehosophat's story
- Testimony Period
- Read Hebrews 10 (Message Bible) and
- 1 John 5:14, 15
- Review of Documents
- Instructions for Courtroom scene
- Song
- Short prayer by all Moms

COURTROOM: (PETITION)

- SONG – "All Rise"
- Invitation to Court
- Attorney's Presentation
- Witnesses to take the Stand
- Attorney's Closing Remarks
- Judge retires to consider Petition
- Signing and Sealing of Documents
- SONG – "Whatever You Ask For in Prayer"

COURTROOM: (THANKSGIVING)

- Read Philippians 5:18
- Each witness (Moms) give thanks verbally through prayer or texts
- Read 1 Peter 5:6, 10, 11
- Thanksgiving Prayer

- SONG – "Thanks, Thanks, I Give You Thanks"
- Pass out Judge's written response
- Listen to Judge's verbal response
- Follow Matthew 8:4 – Tell no one until God gives permission

COURTROOM: (CELEBRATION)

- SONG – "Let My Life Praise You"
- Reading – Faith to Faith
- Break Bread Together
- Closing

INSTRUCTIONS TO MOMS FOR COURT ROOM:
1. Prepare to literally meet the Lord himself on this day. Dress accordingly.
2. Be assured that the Lord himself will inhabit the assigned seats/robes. You may not see Him, but know that He is there.
3. When you take the stand, address your remarks directly to the Judge
4. Set all documents in front of you – Have extra pages for notes
5. Open praise – feel free to respond to the Spirit
6. Everything said or done should be confidential.

CHAPTER 8
OUR DAY IN COURT

Friday came – it seems all too quickly! Were we ready for this incredible meeting? Would it actually come together as we had anticipated? What would actually happen once we got in the room? These questions were racing through my mind like a roller coaster. I felt scared, excited, vulnerable but expectant. I couldn't have dreamt up all of this by myself. But I knew it would also be a day of warfare. If God was really working in covenant relationship here, the enemy would do everything possible to see to it that our plans are derailed. I made a last minute phone call to alert everyone – "Expect trouble today – but even if you have to crawl to this court session this evening – don't miss this meeting."

Chores seemed so intrusive in my schedule for this important day. I had to force myself to think of the mundane things I had to accomplish this Friday before our meeting that evening. One thing I had forgotten was that my car was due for a service that very morning – the last thing I wanted to do was go out of the house, but I had no choice. Quickly dragging on my clothes, I cranked up the engine and headed toward the car dealership – a full briefcase of material that I could review while waiting accompanied me on the front seat. It was critical that all the documents be labeled and organized correctly for a smooth flow. I utilized my waiting time efficiently with prayer and review of the documents. Just as I was breathing a sigh of relief that all was in order, I heard my name over the intercom for completion of service. Perfect timing! Now I could get home and begin to gather the items necessary for decorating the court room.

The rumble of the engine couldn't compare with the rumble of my stomach – I was running on gas of my own! Leaving the parking lot and turning right to merge with oncoming traffic, my eyes seemed a bit hazy. Maybe I was just very tired. I wiped them then looked again. No, I was not just tired – indeed smoke was coming out from the hood of my car! I quickly pulled over on the side ramp. Before I could think, the smoke was coming up thick and black and something told me I should get out of the car. I did, and ran a few feet away – shocked and confused, because NOTHING was wrong with the car when I brought it in for regular service. This was not the day of cell phones, so my only option was to run back 3 blocks to let the attendant know that they needed to come and pick up the car to have it checked again.

It was on my way back that I paused and reflected – this was a DISTRACTION – a situation sent to disquiet my spirit, disrupt my plans for the day and ultimately hinder this petition process! OH NO – This will not happen today! I was determined to take my own advice – crawl to the courtroom if I had to. Another few hours of waiting went by as they towed the car and had it checked again. This time I'm reinforcing my mind with these words, "NOTHING – NOTHING will keep me away from meeting with you today Lord!"

The Lord knew what we all were going through that day – one lady fell down the stairs at home – she just fell and didn't know how she fell, but was determined to come with a crutch if she had too. Everyone had their personal challenge that day, but the hours kept ticking away and we knew that with God's help it would soon be time to meet with Him. Later that day, I received a call from one of the ladies asking if she could bring someone else to the meeting with her. This totally threw me off track. We had discussed so many times the importance of keeping this private and emphasized the study required before the date – to think of bringing a strange person into it at this point was unheard of. Besides, God had chosen the people who should be involved – not me. Of course, I had to say a firm NO, and that disturbed both her feelings and mine. The enemy would try anything to shatter this – and I MUST keep my attitude in check.

I began to get dressed and, for the first time in life, I kept scrutinizing everything I put on, asking myself if Jesus would approve of this item. I guess I should have been that thoughtful of his likes and dislikes all my life. When you're going to meet the King, everything has to be just right! My car was finally loaded with all the items needed on my list.

Taking a deep breath, I called the girls together. Holding back the tears in my eyes, I said "This is THE MOST IMPORTANT MEETING I will ever attend, and it will be the most important day of your life. Daddy will stay with you and go over your new names and the meaning of those names. Try to remember all he shares with you, for this is who you will become in Christ once this adoption petition is over."

From the looks on their faces, I knew this was too much for them to comprehend fully. But I knew that as they grew older, time would confirm the significance of this day. I can't remember ever being this excited or this scared!

I got there with more than enough time to set up the room-antique chairs were used for seating for the Father, Son and Holy Spirit and their judge's robes were draped on each chair. All was ready, but my mind was haunted by the thought that I was really going crazy! Downstairs in the lobby, we all met at the appointed time. I was so shocked by the immaculate attire and grooming of each lady. They had taken this just as seriously as I had, they were here to meet with their Lord. Everyone was on time except the one person whose request I had to deny earlier that day. The Lord whispered in my ear, "Go ahead Brenda – she isn't coming." That was the saddest moment of this experience, the enemy won in excluding her and who knows what type of loss she would experience by being disobedient. I couldn't let the sadness overwhelm me. God was still in control and He was awaiting the presentation of our petition to Him.

We assembled in the ante-chambers. It seemed like no one was even breathing. We reviewed the procedure for the evening and before I could finish, the flood gates opened and tears broke forth like rain. I confessed that the enemy kept taunting me with words of ridicule – this is stupid – it's a silly game and you would be sorry for having subjected these intelligent women to such a ridiculous proposal. But they all confirmed that we've come too far together and they believed that God was going to do something miraculous for us that evening.

"PRAY," the Spirit whispered, and we did. Then, taking a deep breath, we filed out one by one down the hallway to the designated Courtroom. Silently we filed in, taking our respective seats on either side of the judges' chairs. When we were settled, the music began – "ALL RISE to stand before the throne in the presence of a Holy GOD." Suddenly the room was transformed – my heart stood still – my body seemed like a shell and I was not sure that what I was sensing was real. This must be what people refer to as an "out of body experience." But one by one each lady stood up, some crying and some with heads bowed. It was obvious they were experiencing something as real as I sensed it. The Trinity – Father, Son, and Holy Spirit – walked in the room and took their seats in the judges' chairs. No one dared to look directly at those chairs. Court was in session and the witnesses were called one by one to present their cases for the adoption of their children. Some kneeled while others fell prostrate, most with tears and earnest pleadings for their children and their needs. "HELP GOD – MY CHILDREN NEED NEW PARENTS!" We also indicated the new name we wanted them to have based on the new character we would like them to possess. I wept with each mother – overwhelmed by the very presence of God.

When it was time for the closing argument, my nerves were frazzled. I was so grateful that my written document contained only the words of God promises (the mind of the judge) to be presented back to Him. How comforting to know that I didn't have to convince the Godhead to do this adoption based on my own convincing words – it would have failed before I began. But God's words are alive and powerful – He knows what He already promised to give to us – so why would He withhold any good thing from us? Somehow, I was confident that by declaring the words of God (the mind of the Judge), this would be a done deal!

The courtroom was silent as we listened for the Verdict. The voice we heard truly sounded as the mighty voice of God – He would agree to adopt our children, because of our faith!! We eagerly completed the adoption papers for each family. Then, we used a red stamp to indicate the agreement was ratified by the blood of Jesus. It said, "PAID IN FULL." Each child now had a new name and a new parent – God himself, and we were now relieved of the burden of raising our children.

With grateful hearts we said "thank you" in the best way we knew how. Then, like the disciples, we broke our fast by breaking bread together – hardly speaking, but with a glow of rejoicing – we had just experienced the very presence of God and lived to share the story!

Excited we were, but before we left strict orders were given as in Bible days – Go, and tell no one what you have seen or heard. I couldn't understand that directive. Isn't this an experience that could encourage moms and parents everywhere to pray for God to adopt their children? Why the silence? We didn't know, but we pledged as a group to seal our lips. I knew that at some point – when God was ready – He would allow me to write about this miraculous experience. But only when He said YES.

It would take years for me to understand the reason for the silence. God needed to complete this testimony by proving that he actually did adopted the children and was functioning as their new parent. TIME was needed to solidify that proof.

Testimony without proof could result in ridicule and disbelief of the miracle of God.

It was dark by the time I got out to my car – only to discover I had a parking ticket posted on my windshield for $120.00 even though the campus was closed for summer break and all spaces were empty! That's just how angry the enemy was that he lost the case that evening. It didn't phase me any. I folded the ticket and put it away, still rejoicing that my children were now adopted by God and He would be responsible for raising them. Nothing could block the flow of my JOY in the Lord!!

CHAPTER 9

10 YEAR FOLLOW-UP PLAN

Months went by and every Mother's eye was focused on her child – anxious to see just what type of changes would take place as a result of our faith effort in going through the adoption petition. If we ran into each other at the mall, church, or grocery store there was only one question on our minds – have you seen any changes yet?

It was not very long before I began to receive thank you cards or calls from mothers confirming that this prayer/petition (as crazy as it may seem) was the best thing that happened to us. The results were so phenomenal is some cases that the Holy Spirit instructed me to come up with a follow up plan for praying for our children on a continuous basis. If one session of prayer could produce such startling results, think what a lifetime of prayer could do for them!! Not sure how to proceed, I took it to the Lord in prayer and, once again, He revealed the plan to me.

COMPLETE COVERAGE – 24/7

The Spirit devised a plan for prayer coverage for our children every day of the week for every day of their lives. Each Mom would be assigned a specific day that would be their "Day of Prayer" for the children. During that 24 hour period, it would be their responsibility to lift up each child – name be name – and intercede on their behalf. A list was drawn up with the name of each child and each Mom indicated the immediate need or concerns for that child which we should be addressing in our prayers. If an emergency or important event came up, they would notify the group of Moms so that we could update and adjust our prayer requests as needed.

Graduations, weddings, child birth, stumbling blocks, crisis times – the children know that they can send in requests to the Moms and we will pray them through. Like bees zoom in on a hive, we focused in prayer on the issues, never having a doubt that it would be resolved – for these are not our children, but God's. This plan allowed our children to be covered in prayer 24 hours a day, seven days a week for as long as we felt it was needed.

As you can guess, we have decided never to quit or vary our prayer schedule. My prayer day for the children is Friday – and the few times I may have missed my prayer appointment, it felt as though I left our children open to a firing squad from the enemy!! This has become one of the MOST important prayer times in each of our lives – especially as we began to see the amazing results in our children (who we now call God's adopted children).

I have had the pleasure of keeping track of their progress over the past ten years. I can assure you God has His hands on each child and is taking exceptionally good care of them. I cannot tell you they are perfect young people with no problems or no issues, but we continue to see how God takes everything in their lives and works it together for their good – maturing them into responsible, successful, spiritual heirs of the King! Instead of runny-nosed brats, we now see organized, well-rounded, mature citizens – doctors, lawyers, business men and women, musicians, physical therapists, military personnel, teachers, administrators, computer analysts – most with advanced degrees. Our last graduate from college will be this year. What a blessing!! We are grateful, not just because they are progressive young adults, but also because the Lord has also honored our prayers for each one for suitable spouses and the ability to pass on this legacy to their children. Each mother, I am sure, will agree that the most exciting and gratifying result of our petition is that they are all solid Christians in the faith. No Mom can ask for anything more!!

So why share this crazy project with the world? Why document something that can easily be interpreted as "make believe?" The words speak for themselves – because it has made strong believers out of us Moms. Having lived through these years and seeing what God has done, we can only impress upon you the truth of the songwriter:

Tis so sweet to trust in Jesus
Just to take Him at His word
Just to rest upon His promise
Just to know 'Thus saith the Lord'

Jesus, Jesus, how we trust Him
How we've proved Him over and over
Jesus, Jesus, precious Jesus
Oh for grace to trust Him more!

Our prayer from the power of this testimony is that you believe with all your heart that Jesus is still real and still performs miracles when we cry out to Him. He is faithful and can be trusted with every part of our lives and everything that belongs to us. I know that He also deals with us according to our personalities and our stages of life. God may save your children in a totally different way. He may never require that you do a petition that seems so "out on a limb," but be assured that He will ask you to do <u>something</u> at some point in your life that indicates your faith and trust in Him.

For without Faith it is impossible to please God, for He that cometh to Him MUST BELIEVE that He is a REWARDER of them who DILIGENTLY SEEK HIM. Please note that He is a REWARDER when you seek after Him with all your heart and soul. This Petition was birthed out of a heart searching after God for His divine intervention and help. I can assure you that before you call, He will answer and while you are yet speaking, He will hear you. Be encouraged – keep asking in faith and wait on the Lord, for it is with the help of the twins – Faith and Patience – that you will inherit the promise.

www.ingramcontent.com/pod-product-compliance
Lightning Source LLC
Chambersburg PA
CBHW061510040426
42450CB00008B/1552